A SWEDISH CHRISTMAS

Simple Scandinavian Crafts, Recipes and Decorations

CAROLINE WENDT AND PERNILLA WÄSTBERG

Translated by Eileen Laurie
First published in Swedish as *Jul: med glitter, godis och grönt*
by Forma Books AB in 2012
First published in English by Floris Books in 2013

British Library CIP data available
ISBN 978-178250-015-5
Printed in Singapore

Contents

Foreword

A homemade present is always a little bit special. You can find fun objects at flea markets to upcycle, explore the great abundance of nature, or work with beautiful yarns and create something completely new. I have always loved working with my hands. In my work as a journalist, however, I rarely have much opportunity to do the things I enjoy. I started working with photographer Pernilla Wästberg and it turned out we had the same interests – reinventing old things and making personalised presents, not just buying them. We started writing about and photographing our projects. Christmas is the season for arts and crafts, and the number of projects just kept on growing – until it became this book.

You will discover many wonderful Christmas projects in this book, using all kinds of materials and techniques: some are very quick; others take a little longer. Learn how to make indoor and outdoor items, food for the Christmas dinner table or decorations for the Christmas tree. Make gifts and discover new ways to make your home cosier. The projects all have one thing in common: they are fun to do. Christmas crafts are not chores; they are projects to enjoy.

A note on crochet terminology

Crochet terminology is different in the UK and US ('double crochet' in the UK is called 'single crochet' in the US). This book is written in UK terminology, with US terminology given in brackets at the start of each pattern.

Enjoy the Festive Feast!

* You don't need Grandma's dinner service to present your Christmas dinner beautifully. Decorate the table using red, green, brown and white. Set the table with plates in different styles for an original look. Find plates at flea markets or online.

* Make candle lanterns with cake doilies. Place a candleholder in the middle of the cake doily and fold up the edges evenly. Tie a colourful ribbon around. Be very careful that the doily doesn't catch fire. Never leave naked flames unattended.

* Cover Styrofoam or polystyrene balls in moss, winding thin, gold thread around to tie it in place.

* Easy as pie! Little gifts make perfect place cards – two jobs in one.

Do you have guests who would get on well together? Or – be honest now – are there others you would rather keep apart? Carefully considering your table plan can be important! Make your place settings special using elves' woolly hats, gingerbread men, sweets or little parcels as place cards. Your guests will love it.

Find your gingerbread man!

Materials: gingerbread men, icing, greaseproof paper and pins or a piping bag

Icing
1 egg white
A few drops of vinegar
250–300 g (1–1¼ cups) icing sugar

Instructions
1. Mix the ingredients for the icing together to reach piping consistency. Add more icing sugar if the mixture is too runny.
2. If you do not have a piping bag, make a cornet out of greaseproof paper and secure with a pin to stop it unravelling.
3. Fill the cornet with the icing mixture. Cut off the tip of the cornet.
4. Pipe the name of each guest in icing onto a gingerbread man.

More place card possibilities

* Make small Christmas crackers and add the name of your guest for the perfect place card.

* Buy small clothes pegs and pots of paint from a craft supplier. Paint each clothes peg and use it to attach a place card to each guest's glass.

* Santa's elves show guests to their seats. Put a woolly elf hat on each glass. If you don't have time to knit the hats yourself, you can buy knitted fabric ready-made from a craft supplier. Simply cut it to the right size and tie on the name card with a piece of string.

* If you like things plain and simple, attach a flower and a name card with a piece of string to each guest's cutlery.

* Vintage Christmas-tree baubles are so colourful they deserve a place at the table. Attach a name card so that your guests can find their seats.

* Be the perfect host or hostess and welcome your guests with a sweet treat. Especially popular with younger guests, such a tasty place card might encourage them to sit still! Buy ready-made bags or sew your own using transparent fabric. Write the names on the bags using a permanent gold marker or fabric paint.

You could buy a dinner service especially for Christmas, but if you like crafts, why not be inventive? Decorating dinnerware with your own designs is much more fun. We painted on Christmas trees, little men and women, stars and hearts in gingerbread colours.

Festive dinnerware

Materials: plates, nail scissors, transparency film or sheets of plastic, porcelain paint, sponge dauber, scalpel, craft knife or sharp knife

Instructions
1. Carefully clean the plates.
2. Cut out stencils using the transparency film. Copy the figures on page 127 or create your own.
3. Hold the stencil steady on the plate and use the sponge dauber to fill the required area with paint. Paint the figures freehand if you are feeling artistic.
4. Leave the paint to dry. (Follow the porcelain paint instructions.)
5. Remove any paint runs once the paint has dried (some porcelain paints may need to be set in the oven). A small, sharp knife can work wonders.

Vintage saucers are very cheap at flea markets, and upcycling them is a real pleasure. We added candleholder bases to our flea-market finds to make beautiful candlesticks.

Candle saucers

Materials: saucers, candleholder bases from a craft supplier, porcelain glue, candles and decorative ribbon

Instructions
1. Glue the candleholder bases firmly to the saucers. Make sure you use an adhesive suitable for porcelain to ensure that the candle is stable.
2. Put the candle into the base and tie a decorative ribbon around it. Be careful to tie the ribbon below the top of the candleholder base – and always keep an eye on lit candles.

Santa's elves ('tomtes' in Swedish) are a hit at the buffet table. Made from decorated toothpicks, they are easy as pie!

Tomte toothpicks

Materials: toothpicks, red nail varnish, fine marker pen

Instructions
1. Dip the tip of each toothpick into the nail varnish. Stand the toothpicks to dry in a thick slice of bread.
2. Carefully draw eyes and mouths with the marker pen.

TIP!

Use the little elves to serve meatballs, chipolata sausages, canapés, dates, figs or chocolates.

Gingerbread men are excellent assistants when it's time for Christmas baking.

Gingerbread-man pot holder

Materials: 100% cotton yarn (UK: 4 ply, US: sport weight): 2 x 50 g (1¾ oz) balls in brown and a small amount of white
Crochet hook: 3.50 mm (UK: 9, US: E–4)
Crochet instructions: begin every row in chain stitch (ch) except for the increase rows. Increase stitches by crocheting the stated number of ch at the end of the row. Work the next row in double (US: single) crochet (dc), beginning with the second ch from the crochet hook.

Chain 31 stitches
Row 1: turn and work 30 dc, beginning with the second ch from hook.
R 2: work 30 dc. Work 6 ch at the end of the row.
R 3: turn and work in dc from the second ch. You now have 35 dc stitches in the row. Work 6 ch at the end of the row.
R 4: work 40 dc. Work 3 ch at the end of the row.
R 5: work 42 dc. Work 3 ch at the end of the row.
R 6–15: work 44 dc.
R 16: skip final dc stitch = 43 dc. Turn.
R 17: skip final dc stitch = 42 dc. Turn.
R 18–27: work 42 dc.
R 28–43: work in dc, but skip final dc stitch on every row = 26 stitches in row 43.
R 44–48: work 26 dc.
R 49: work 26 dc. Work 10 ch at the end of the row.
R 50: work 35 dc. Work 10 ch at the end of the row.
R 51–55: work 44 dc.
R 56–67: skip final dc stitch = 32 dc in row 67.
R 68: work 23 dc. Turn.
R 69: work 14 dc. Turn.
R 70–73: skip final dc stitch on all rows = 10 dc in row 73.
R 74: work 10 dc.
R 75: work 10 dc. Work 2 ch at the end of the row.
R 76: work 11 dc. Work 2 ch at the end of the row.
R 77: work 12 dc. Work 2 ch at the end of the row.
R 78: work 13 dc. Work 2 ch at the end of the row.
R 79–82: work 14 dc.
R 83–88: skip final dc stitch in every row = 8 dc.
Fasten off.

Finishing: Crochet in brown round the edges of the gingerbread man. Work 1 dc in every dc stitch and in every row. You might need 3 dc in the corner stitch for the large curved parts. You might need to skip 1 dc in the smaller curved parts. Work 2 rows in brown. Fasten off. Create a loop by chaining 20 stitches, beginning with a stitch in the middle of the gingerbread man's head. Tightly work the final stitch of the loop into the same stitch on the gingerbread man's head. Turn and work 25 dc around the loop. Turn and work 1 dc in every dc stitch in the loop. Cut the yarn and fasten off. Work in slip stitch in white between the two rows in brown around the entire gingerbread man. Hold the yarn at the back and take stitches from the front, 1 slip stitch in every dc. Embroider the text in ch. Weave in all loose ends.

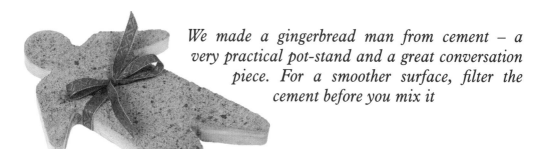

We made a gingerbread man from cement – a very practical pot-stand and a great conversation piece. For a smoother surface, filter the cement before you mix it

Gingerbread-man pot stand

Materials: cement, large gingerbread-man cutter, oil, flat wooden board (or similar), floor-protector pads or felt backing, gloves to protect your hands, double-sided tape, little wooden block, an old spoon.

Instructions
1. Mix the cement according to the instructions on the packet.
2. Place the gingerbread man cutter on the wooden board or other suitable flat base that you don't mind getting scratched and dirty. Grease the surface and the cutter with oil. Tape the cutter to the base using double-sided tape.
3. Pour the cement into the cutter until it almost reaches the top edge. Smooth the surface. Push the surface down gently with a little wooden block to remove all air bubbles, and then use a spoon to smooth it.
4. Leave to dry for two days somewhere cool.
5. Carefully remove the cutter.
6. Attach self-adhesive floor-protector pads or similar protective felt backing to the underside of the gingerbread man.

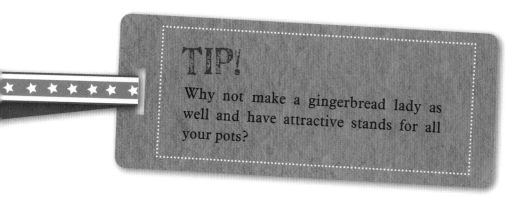

TIP!

Why not make a gingerbread lady as well and have attractive stands for all your pots?

Making sweets is a Christmas highlight – my favourites are caramels. Homemade caramel bars make a sweet treat for the whole family and are also lovely gifts. Make several batches to be sure you really have enough.

Caramel bars

Ingredients
100 g (3½ oz) brown sugar
150 g (5¼ oz) castor sugar
150 ml (⅔ cup) glucose
2 tablespoons golden syrup
100 ml (just less than ½ cup) whipping cream
pinch of salt

Instructions
1. Mix all the ingredients in a saucepan with a heavy base (not aluminium). Boil for about 20 minutes until the mixture has reached 121°C (250°F). Use a cooking thermometer to check the temperature. If you don't have a cooking thermometer, you can try the cold water test: pour a little of the caramel mixture into cold water. When the mixture forms a ball, the caramel is ready to pour.
2. Pour the mixture into a 25 x 15 cm (10 x 6 in) baking tray lined with baking paper. Leave to harden.
3. Cut the caramel into pieces using oiled scissors or a knife. If you make the bars the same size as those in the photograph, you will have around 25.

We wrapped up our caramels like little Christmas crackers – really sweet and really easy. A lovely gift.

Cute caramel crackers

Materials: baking paper, string or ribbon, coloured paper (e.g. wrapping paper or coloured sheets of paper), sticky tape

Instructions
1. Cut the baking paper into small pieces and wrap the caramel bars leaving the paper long at the ends. Cut the string or ribbon into short lengths and tie around the ends of the paper like Christmas crackers.
2. Cut the wrapping paper (or coloured paper) into sections and wrap them around the caramel crackers. Finish by taping a small strip of contrasting paper around the middle.

It's lovely to give unusual gifts – like the ingredients for biscuits. Put the dry ingredients in a jar and tie on the recipe.

Cookies in a jar

Materials: glass jar, ribbon, two crocheted doilies or circles of pretty fabric, a decorative card

Ingredients
500 g (1 lb) plain flour
300 g (10½ oz) light muscovado sugar
2 teaspoons cinnamon
½ teaspoon baking powder
150 g (5 oz) dark chocolate drops (or pieces of chocolate)
150 g (5 oz) shelled pistachios

Instructions
1. Put the dry ingredients in the glass jar in layers.
2. Place the two crocheted doilies or circles of pretty fabric on the lid of the jar and tie the ribbon around them. Write this recipe on the card:
   Mix together the contents of the jar with 200 g (7 oz) of butter at room temperature, 1 teaspoon of vanilla extract and 2 eggs. Using your hands, divide the mixture into rough balls and place on a baking tray. Bake for 8–10 minutes in the oven at 175°C (350°F). This makes around 30 biscuits.
3. Attach the card to the jar with a ribbon.

Gingerbread and Christmas: a classic flavour, taste and look. A gingerbread basket is full of festive cheer. Perfect for all you sweet-toothed people – when all the sweets are gone you can eat the basket!

Gingerbread basket

Materials: gingerbread dough (ready-made or your own recipe), oven gloves, castor sugar, plate, round jar, icing sugar, vinegar, egg white, edible silver balls

Instructions

1. Roll out the dough. Cut out the round base, using a plate or similar as a template.
2. For the sides, measure the circumference of the base and halve this measurement. Cut out two pieces of dough this length and 7–10 cm (3–4 in) high. Cut the top edge into a wave shape or zigzag with a knife.
3. Cut out a piece of dough for the handle.
4. Put all the pieces on a baking tray and bake in the oven. Reduce the temperature of the oven a little from your usual gingerbread recipe and bake the dough for a little longer, so that it becomes harder and doesn't shrink too much.
5. Mould the pieces into the required shape as soon as you take them out of the oven. They will still be very warm so use oven gloves. Shape the side section and the handle using a round jar or similar and leave the gingerbread pieces to cool. It is a bit tricky and it might take a few attempts to get the shapes right.
6. Melt some sugar in a frying pan on a medium heat and use the liquid sugar to stick the pieces together. Be very careful as the sugar will be extremely hot.
7. Mix one egg white, some drops of vinegar and 250 g (½ lb) icing sugar. Add more icing sugar if needed to reach piping consistency. Decorate by piping on the icing and adding silver balls.

Classic Christmas gingerbread men can be decorative too...

Gingerbread-man wreath

Materials: 8 gingerbread men, icing (see recipe on page 9), glue, 1½ m
(5 ft) ribbon

Instructions
1. Place four gingerbread men in a ring with their feet towards the centre.
2. Use the glue gun to stick four more gingerbread men on top of the bottom four.
3. Decorate the gingerbread men with icing.
4. Wrap the ribbon around the gingerbread men as shown in the photograph. Tie a bow and hang up.

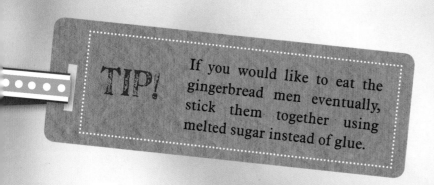

TIP! If you would like to eat the gingerbread men eventually, stick them together using melted sugar instead of glue.

Cushion moss is very attractive and helps non-florists like us make beautiful decorations. A jar of homemade breadsticks, surrounded by cushion moss, can make a considerate gift if you're invited to someone's home.

A festive jar

Materials: deep dish or bowl, glass jar, cushion moss, ivy, string or ribbon, glass balls, silver pins or other small decorations, breadsticks (see recipe on page 38)

Instructions
1. Decorate the jar with attractive ribbon or string.
2. Place the jar in the middle of the dish.
3. Arrange pieces of cushion moss around the jar. Divide up strands of ivy and place between the pieces of moss until the entire dish is covered with moss and ivy.
4. Decorate with glass balls, silver pins or similar (you probably have decorations at home).
5. Put the breadsticks in the jar.

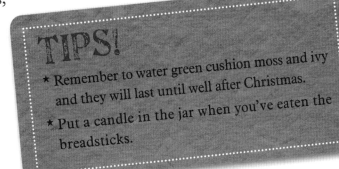

TIPS!
★ Remember to water green cushion moss and ivy and they will last until well after Christmas.
★ Put a candle in the jar when you've eaten the breadsticks.

These breadsticks are simply delicious. Sunflower and poppy seeds make them extra-special.

Pernilla's breadsticks

Ingredients
50 g (1¾ oz) fresh bread yeast
100 g (3½ oz) butter
500 ml (½ quart) buttermilk
1 tablespoon salt
75 ml (⅓ cup) treacle
400 g (14 oz) plain flour plus 100 g
   (3½ oz) for kneading

400 g (14 oz) spelt flour
400 g (14 oz) wholewheat flour
400 g (14 oz) coarse rye flour
400–500 g (14–17½ oz) sunflower
   seeds
50 g (1¾ oz) black poppy seeds

Instructions
1. Crumble the yeast into a bowl.
2. Melt the butter and add the buttermilk to the saucepan. Heat the liquid to 37°C (100°F) and add it to the yeast in the bowl.
3. Add the salt, treacle, the four types of flour and 150 g (5 oz) of the sunflower seeds. Knead all ingredients to a smooth dough, cover with a tea towel and leave to rise for around 50 minutes. Heat the oven to 225°C (450°F) (or 200°C (400°F)in a fan oven).
4. Place the dough on a floured surface and divide into four sections. Roll out each section and cut into strips of around 3 x 18 cm (1 x 7 in). This will make around 80 breadsticks. Brush with plenty of water and sprinkle over the sunflower and poppy seeds. Press the seeds in gently with your hands.
5. Place the breadsticks on a baking tray and bake for around 10 minutes or until they are golden brown. Leave them to cool on a wire baking rack. If you would like crispier breadsticks, bake them for several hours (preferably in a fan oven) at 40°C (100°F).

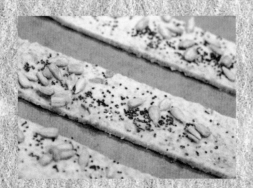

Time to Relax

Christmas celebrations are a lot of fun, but just sitting down and relaxing with a book or a crossword is also wonderful.

What could be better than curling up on the sofa with this Christmas crafts book? I need a soft case for my reading glasses – why not make it candy–striped? It's very easy to knit this glasses case and then felt it in the washing machine.

Candy-striped glasses case

Materials: untreated woollen felting yarn (UK: DK, US: light worsted) in white (50 g, 1¾ oz) and red (20 g, ¾ oz)
Needles: 6–8 mm (UK: 4–0, US: 10–11); knit very loosely

Instructions

1. Cast on 30 stitches in white using the two-strand method (also called the long-tail method). Work in stocking stitch. Follow the pattern on page 126. Knit with a single strand of yarn, using white for the pale sections and red for the shaded sections. Work 30 rows. Cast off and weave in all loose ends.
2. Machine wash the case at 60°C (140°F). Select a normal wash programme (no pre-wash) with a spin cycle. Use washing powder and add a bath towel to assist the felting process. If the case is not completely felted, wash it again. The actual size of the final case depends on the washing temperature and amount of powder used.
3. Gently mould the case to the required size and shape. Make sure the edges are straight.
4. Sew together one short side and one long side.

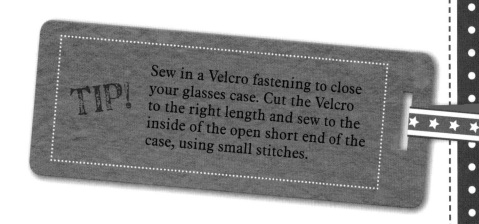

TIP! Sew in a Velcro fastening to close your glasses case. Cut the Velcro to the right length and sew to the inside of the open short end of the case, using small stitches.

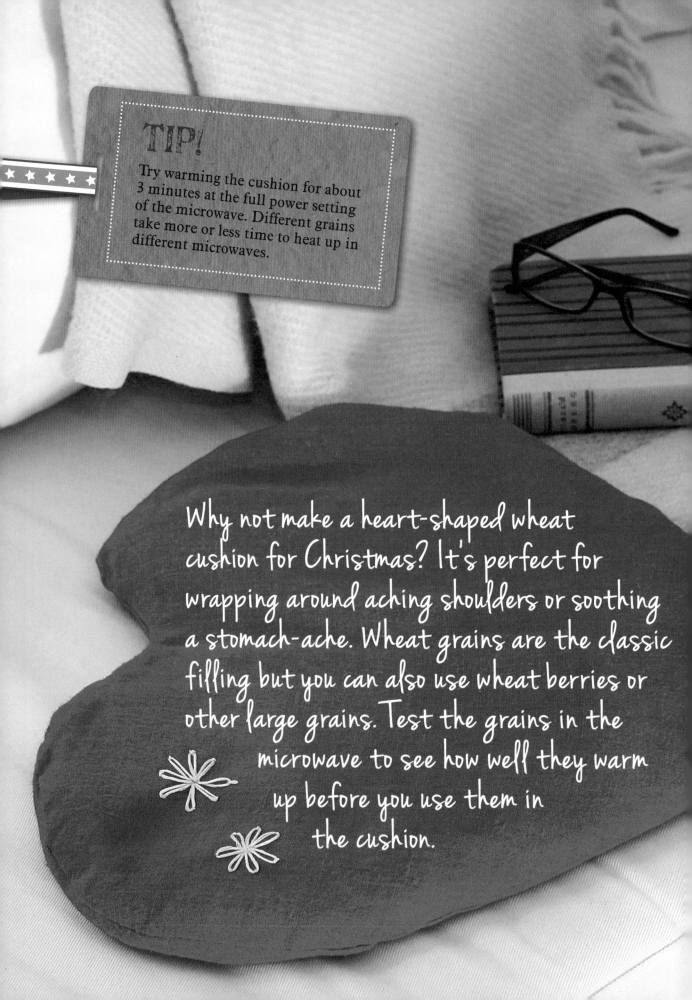

TIP!

Try warming the cushion for about 3 minutes at the full power setting of the microwave. Different grains take more or less time to heat up in different microwaves.

Why not make a heart-shaped wheat cushion for Christmas? It's perfect for wrapping around aching shoulders or soothing a stomach-ache. Wheat grains are the classic filling but you can also use wheat berries or other large grains. Test the grains in the microwave to see how well they warm up before you use them in the cushion.

Warming wheat cushion

Materials: 80 x 50 cm (30 x 20 in) piece of red linen; 80 x 50 cm (30 x 20 in) piece of cotton, e.g. an old bed sheet; linen or cotton yarn; 2 kg (4½ lb) wheat berries, wheat grains or similar; a large piece of paper

Instructions

1. Make a heart template using the paper. This heart is about 40 cm (16 in) long and 35 cm (14 in) wide.
2. Use the template for cutting two pieces of cotton and two pieces of linen.
3. Sew the cotton pieces together, right sides facing, leaving a 10 cm (4 in) wide opening. Do the same with the linen pieces, leaving a 20 cm (8 in) wide opening.
4. Turn the sewn pieces right sides out and press.
5. Fill the cotton heart with the grains. Sew up the opening using small neat stitches, by hand or sewing machine.
6. Embroider flowers onto the red linen heart using the yarn.
7. Place the cotton inner piece inside the linen piece. Sew up the opening using neat stitches.

White fabric doilies on a dark blanket really do look like snowflakes!

Snowflake blanket

Materials: blanket, needle and white thread, pins, round crocheted or lace doilies from a flea market

Instructions

1. Position and pin the doilies on the blanket.
2. Sew onto the blanket using small, firm stitches.

The snowflake pattern on this cushion will give a room that festive feeling, and the cushion is comfortable and cosy.

Snowflake cushion cover

Materials: 3 balls of red and 1 ball of white yarn (UK: aran, US: worsted weight)
Gauge: 14 stitches over 20 rows = 10 cm (4 in)
Needles: 5.5 mm (UK: 5, US: 9) or change to fit gauge
Cushion size: 37 x 37 cm (14½ x 14½ in) (You will need a cushion to fill the cover.)

Instructions
Cast on 49 stitches in red. Work in stocking stitch, starting with a knit row. Start the snowflake pattern in row 17 (see pattern page 126). On rows 17–45, work 10 stitches in stocking stitch, follow the pattern for 29 stitches and finish with 10 stitches in stocking stitch. Continue until the snowflake pattern is complete. Work 77 more rows in stocking stitch in red – 122 rows in total. Weave in all loose ends and press both sides lightly. Fold and sew up two sides, right sides facing, and leave one edge open. Turn right side out and put the cushion pad into the knitted cover. Sew up the final edge with small, neat stitches.

TIP!

Knitting a design in two colours one stitch at a time can be tricky. Pull the yarn firmly but not too tightly across the back of the work. With longer lengths of yarn it's a good idea to wind the yarn around a bobbin – or to cut the yarn and have a separate length for the stitches at the edges. Take care to keep the snowflake flat.

You can make these cute little elves by knitting in stocking stitch. Knit on large needles and then let the washing machine do the hard work. The best part of the felting process is when you open the washing machine – it feels like opening a Christmas present.

Santa's elves are coming to town!

Materials: 100% wool yarn or felting yarn (UK: DK, US: light worsted weight) in grey and red – 1 ball of each colour will make 5 large elves and 4 small ones; white and pink unspun wool; cotton wool; large buttons or wooden discs
Needles: 6 mm (UK: 4, US: 10)

Instructions

1. Small elf (large elf): cast on 14 (20) stitches in grey. Work 4 (6) rows in stocking stitch in grey. Change to red and continue in stocking stitch for another 6 (8) rows. Now begin decreasing by knitting 2 stitches together 3 (4) times, divided evenly across a knit row. Repeat decreases 4 times on knit rows. Work 6 rows. Cast off.
2. Sew the long edge of the elf together with a piece of yarn before you begin felting. Sew with small stitches from the right side.
3. Wash the elves in the washing machine at 60°C (140°F). Select a normal wash programme (no pre-wash) with a spin cycle. Use washing powder and put a bath towel in the washing machine along with the elves. If the elves are not completely felted, wash again. Once the felting process is completed, stretch and shape the elves to the correct size.
4. Add the cotton-wool filling. Make a solid, flat base by 'darning' in grey, working first from top to bottom, and then from left to right, weaving in all loose ends. Felt the noses by dipping small pieces of unspun pink wool in lukewarm soapy water and rolling them into balls. Sew on the noses using small stitches. Sew on pieces of unspun wool or cotton wool for the beards. Make the elves more stable by gluing them onto large buttons or wooden discs.

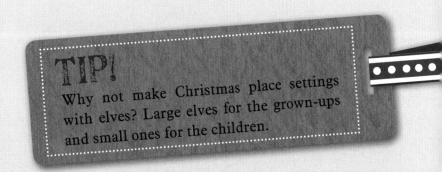

TIP!

Why not make Christmas place settings with elves? Large elves for the grown-ups and small ones for the children.

I have lots of plain white plant pots at home — classic but a bit dull. As I loveknitting, I made them some woollen plant pot covers.

Moss-stitch plant pot cover

Materials: 2 balls 100% wool (UK: aran, US: worsted weight) in light grey
Needles: 5 mm (UK: 6, US: 8)
Size: to fit a plant pot with a circumference of 55 cm (22 in), height 15 cm (6 in)

Instructions
Cast on 66 stitches. Work in moss stitch (knit 1, purl 1 in the first row, and purl 1, knit 1 in the second row). Repeat these 2 rows throughout. You will always have a knit stitch in the row above a purl stitch and vice versa. When the work is 17 cm (6½ in) long, cast off. Weave in loose ends and sew together the short edges from the wrong side.

Red-knit plant pot cover

Materials: use a thick, fluffy, single-stranded yarn (UK: bulky, US: roving) in 100% wool: 2 x 50 g (1¾ oz) balls
Needles: 5 mm (UK: 6, US: 8)
Size: to fit a plant pot with a circumference of 47 cm (18½ in), height 18 cm (7 in)
Stitch pattern
Row 1: knit 2, purl 2.
R 2: knit 2, purl 2 (knit stitches above knit, purl stitches above purl).
R 3: purl 2, knit 2.
R 4: purl 2, knit 2 (purl stitches above purl and knit stitches above knit).

Instructions
Cast on 30 stitches. Follow pattern until the work is 50 cm (20 in) long or the right length for your plant pot. Cast off, weave in loose ends and sew short edges together from the wrong side.

Scandinavian-star plant pot cover

Materials: use a thick sock yarn in grey and undyed
Size: to fit a plant pot with a circumference of 64 cm (25 in), height 17 cm (6½ in)
Needles: short circular needle, 5.5 mm (UK: 5, US: 9)

Instructions

Cast on 128 stitches in grey. Work in stocking stitch for 4 rows. Starting on row 5, follow the snowflake pattern on page 126. Then work 12 rows in stocking stitch in grey. Cast off. Weave in loose ends. Fold up about 4 rows at the bottom edge to make a 'collar' and sew up at the back.

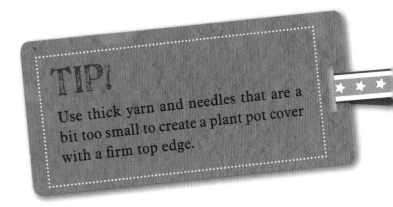

TIP!

Use thick yarn and needles that are a bit too small to create a plant pot cover with a firm top edge.

Felting is easy and fun. Remember to use untreated 100% wool, otherwise the felting will not work.

Crocheted fruit bowl

Materials: 100% wool, grey yarn (UK: chunky, US: craft weight): 2 x 100g (3½ oz) balls; red felt; fabric glue
Crochet hook: 5–6 mm (UK: 6–4, US: H–8–J–10), crochet loosely

Crochet instructions

Cast on 3 chain stitches. Join with 1 slip stitch to make a ring.

Row 1: crochet 6 double (US: single) crochet (dc) around the ring. Begin this and all rows with a chain stitch and join this and all rows with a slip stitch in the first dc stitch in the row.

R 2: work 2 dc in every dc = 12 dc.

R 3: work 2 dc in every dc = 24 dc.

R 4: work *1 dc, work 2 dc in next dc* = 36 dc.

R 5: work 1 dc in every dc = 36 dc.

R 6: work *5 dc, 2 dc in next dc* = 42 dc.

R 7: work *6 dc, 2 dc in next dc* = 48 dc.

R 8: work *7 dc, 2 dc in next dc* = 54 dc.

R 9: work *8 dc, 2 dc in next dc* = 60 dc.

R 10: work *9 dc, work 2 dc in next dc* = 66 dc.

R 11–12: work 1 dc in every dc = 66 dc.

R 13: work *10 dc, skip 1 dc* = 60 dc.

R 14–17: work 1 dc in every dc = 60 dc.

R 18: work *14 dc, skip 1 dc* = 56 dc.

R 19–22: work 1 dc in every dc = 56 dc.

Fasten off. Weave in all loose ends.

Crocheted nut bowl

Materials: thick, fluffy, 100% wool, single-stranded yarn (UK: bulky, US: roving): 2 x 50 g balls in black; small length of untreated, 100% wool, grey yarn; red felt; fabric glue
Crochet hook: 9 mm (US: M), crochet loosely

Crochet instructions
Cast on 3 chain stitches in black; join with 1 slip stitch to make a ring
Rows 1–10: follow instructions for the fruit bowl.
R 11–20: 1 double (US: single) crochet (dc) in every dc = 66 dc. Cut yarn and fasten off.
R 21: change to grey and work 1 row. Cut yarn and fasten off. Weave in all loose ends.

Felting the bowls

Wash the crocheted pieces in the washing machine, add washing powder and use a normal wash programme (no pre-wash) at 60°C (140°F). Spin. Add a bath towel to assist the felting process. If the bowls are not completely felted, wash again. The actual size of the final bowls depends on the washing temperature and amount of powder used. After washing, mould the bowls to the required size and shape. Cut out hearts from the red felt freehand or using a cake cutter as a template. Glue them carefully to the bowls using fabric glue.

The great thing about wrist-warmers is that you can wear them indoors and out. They are simple to knit, even for beginners. All you need is knit and purl. I made several pairs as Christmas gifts – fun to do and always appreciated.

Wrist-warmers

Materials: 1 ball of soft yarn (UK: 4 ply, US: sport weight) in red; a piece of white yarn
Needles: 3 mm (UK: 11, US: 2–3)
Crochet hook: 3 mm (UK: 10, US: C–2–D–3)
Size: to fit an adult woman

Knitting instructions

Cast on 34 stitches in red. Work 28 rows in garter stitch. In row 29, knit 4, purl 26, knit 4. Knit row 30. Continue these last 2 rows for 12 more rows. Then work 28 rows in stocking stitch. Cast off loosely and weave in loose ends. Make the second wrist-warmer in same way.

Embroider 6 crosses in a row in undyed yarn on the stocking stitch section (see photograph). Sew up the wrist-warmers from the wrong side with as little seam allowance as possible.

Crochet edge: begin at the seam. Work 1 double (US: single) crochet (dc) in red in every second row along the edge, but not the last stitch = 34 dc. End with 1 slip stitch in the first dc. Cut yarn. Work in white ★2 dc, 1 dc + 1 treble (US: double) crochet in next dc, 1 treble crochet + 1 dc in next dc★, repeat ★ to ★ 8 times. Cut yarn and weave in all loose ends.

Easy to crochet and fun to wear at Christmas – make friendship bracelets for your family and friends.

Friendship bracelet

Materials: small pieces of 4–ply (US: sport weight) yarn in red, green and white; pretty buttons or glass beads
Crochet hook: 3 mm (UK: 10, US: C–2–D–3)
Sizes: child 16 cm, 6 in (woman 20 cm, 8 in)

Crochet instructions
Chain 37 (43) stitches (ch). Turn and work in double (US: single) crochet (dc), the first stitch in the second dc stitch from the crochet hook. Crochet back across the row, 1 dc in every dc, total stitches 36 (42). Turn corner by working 2 dc in the end stitch, work 1 dc along the side and 2 more dc in the corner stitch, then 1 dc in every dc. Cut yarn after second row of dc. Change yarn. Begin in one corner and work 3 dc on the short edge, make an extra dc in the corner and then work the long edge, 1 dc in every dc. At the next corner, work 2 dc at the corner, 1 dc, 2 dc at the corner and then 1 dc in every dc along the long edge. Work 1 slip stitch (ss) in the first dc. Finish by making a loop. Work 8 ch beginning on one side, join with 1 dc at the second edge on the same side. Finish with 1 ss. Turn and work 9 dc along the ch ring. Finish with 1 ss. Weave in all loose ends.

Finishing
Sew on a button for securing the bracelet. Add pretty buttons or beads as decoration.

You can always buy a nice cushion to brighten up the sofa at Christmas, but we think it's more fun to make your own. This is a lovely way to upcycle embroidered vintage handicrafts.

Upcycled cushions

Materials: cushions in different sizes; single-colour fabrics; patterned and embroidered festive tablecloths, handkerchiefs or embroidered sheets

Instructions

1. Cut 2 pieces of fabric to make the front and back of the cushion cover. For a 40 x 40 cm (16 x 16 in) cushion, cut a piece of fabric that is slightly smaller so the cushion fits snugly inside.
2. Cut zigzag edges on both pieces.
3. Pin your section of embroidered tablecloth or similar found treasures to the front piece. Sew securely by hand or use your sewing machine's straight stitch.
4. Place the front and back pieces together, right sides facing. Pin and sew. Leave an opening on one side large enough to fit in the cushion.
5. Turn the cushion right side out and press.
6. Put the cushion in the cover. Sew up the opening by hand or sewing machine.

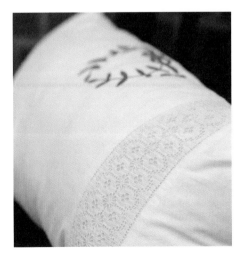

This long-legged Santa with candy-striped arms and legs looks great hanging up on the wall. He'll take good care of your Christmas cards!

Crocheted Santa postman

Materials: cotton yarn suitable for crocheting with a 3.5 mm (UK: 9, US: E–4) crochet hook: 100 g (3½ oz) red, 50 g (1¾ oz) white and 100g (3½ oz) black; cotton wool for filling; embroidery thread for the face; unspun sheep's wool for the beard and hair

Crochet hook: 3.5 mm (UK: 9, US: E–4)
Begin all rows with a chain stitch (ch). When you have crocheted a row, always finish with 1 slip stitch (ss) in the first stitch. This applies to all sections.
Changing yarn: leave the last crochet stitch unfinished with 2 loops on the hook. Pull the new yarn through these 2 loops.

Legs

Cast on 3 ch in white. Join with 1 ss to make a ring.
Row 1: work 6 double (US: single) crochet (dc) around the ring.
R 2–4: 6 dc in white.
R 5: change to red. Increase by working 2 dc in 1 dc = 7 dc.

R 6–8: 7 dc in red.
Now work 4 rows white, 4 rows red. Continue this pattern. Increase 1 stitch in the first row of each colour block until there are 16 dc. Work 15 colour blocks in total and fasten off. Make 2 legs and stuff with cotton wool.

Arms

Make in the same way as the legs, this time with 11 colour blocks. Make 2 arms and stuff with cotton wool.

Body

Chain 29 stitches in red.
R 1: turn and work 28 dc beginning with the second ch from the crochet hook.
R 2: work 27 dc, skip last dc, turn.
R 3: work 26 dc, skip last dc, turn.

Continue decreasing in this way in every row until 6 dc remain.
Make 2 identical pieces. Dc 2 stitches together, 1 dc in every row and stitch. Add filling before crocheting together.

Continues on next page

Head

Chain 6 stitches in white. Join to make a ring.

R 1: crochet 8 dc around the ring.

R 2: work *1 dc, work 2 dc in next dc* = 12 dc.

R 3: work *1 dc, work 2 dc in next dc* = 18 dc.

R 4: work *2 dc, work 2 dc in next dc* = 24 dc.

R 5: work *2 dc, work 2 dc in next dc*, repeat * to * = 32 dc.

R 6: work *7 dc, work 2 dc in next dc*, repeat * to * = 36 dc.

R 7–12: work 36 dc.

R 13: change to red.

R 14–20: work 36 dc.

R 21: work *8 dc, skip 1 dc*, repeat * to * = 32 dc.

R 22–23: work 32 dc.

R 24: work *3 dc, skip 1 dc*, repeat * to * = 24 dc.

R 25-26: work 24 dc. Add filling to head before continuing.

R 27: work *2 dc, skip 1 dc*, repeat * to * = 16 dc.

R 28–40: work 16 dc.

R 41: work *1 dc, skip 1 dc*, repeat * to * = 8 dc.

R 42–52: work 8 dc.

Fasten off. Weave in all loose ends. Pull down Santa's woolly hat and sew to the back of his neck. Sew the arms and legs onto the body. Embroider the eyes in embroidery thread and sew on nose (see instructions below). Sew on lambswool for the beard and hair with grey thread.

Nose

Chain 3 stitches in white. Join with 1 ss to make a ring. Work 1 ch, work 4 dc around the ring. End with 1 ss in the first dc. Cut yarn and fasten off.

Christmas postbag

Chain 37 stitches in black.

Turn and work 36 dc. (Use a postcard to measure the bag to get the right size. Chain more or fewer stitches as required.)

Work 58 rows in total, or the required number to attain the right size.

Fasten off. Weave in all loose ends. Fold over the bag and dc the sides together.

TIP!

Fill Santa's postbag with nuts, small Christmas-tree balls or mystery parcels. Add a piece of cardboard to make the bag more stable.

Red heart

Chain 2 stitches in red.

R 1: turn and work 2 dc, the first stitch in the second dc stitch from crochet hook.

R 2: turn and work 2 dc in every dc = 4 dc.

R 3: turn and work 2 dc in the first and last dc, 1 dc in the remaining stitches = 6 dc.

R 4: work 6 dc.

R 5–16: continue work as follows: 2 dc in the first and last dc in every second row, dc in dc until there are 18 dc in row 16.

R 17–18: work 18 dc.

R 19: work 8 dc. Turn.

R 20: work 8 dc.

R 21–25: decrease 1 stitch in every row by not working the last dc in the row until there are 3 dc left. Cut yarn and fasten off.

Repeat rows 19–25 for the other side of the heart.

Work 1 row in dc around the heart, 1 dc stitch in every row or dc. Fasten off.

Finishing

Sew the heart onto the bag. Sew the back of the bag to Santa's stomach. Weave in all loose ends. Place Santa's arms around the postbag and sew on with invisible stitches to the front of the bag.

We love the fragrance of Christmas spices. Create the festive feeling with these scented tea-towel hearts.

Clove and cinnamon hearts

Materials: tea towels, lace ribbon, Christmas spices like cloves and cinnamon, pine branches, cotton wool for stuffing

Instructions

1. Make a paper template for the heart. Use the template on page 127 or draw your own. Pin the template to a folded tea towel, placing it over the most attractive patterns. Cut out, leaving a 1 cm (½ in) seam allowance.
2. Cut a 15–20 cm (6–8 in) length of lace ribbon.
3. Place the heart pieces together, right sides facing. Double over the lace ribbon and place the ends in between the 2 pieces of fabric. Pin together.
4. Machine sew the hearts together, leaving a 3–4 cm (¾–1 in) opening on one side.
5. Turn the heart right side out. If required, use a pin to push out the seams and corners. Press flat.
6. Add the cotton-wool stuffing and spices to the heart. Sew up the opening by hand using small stitches.
7. Attach 2 cinnamon sticks and a little pine branch to the top of the heart with thread.

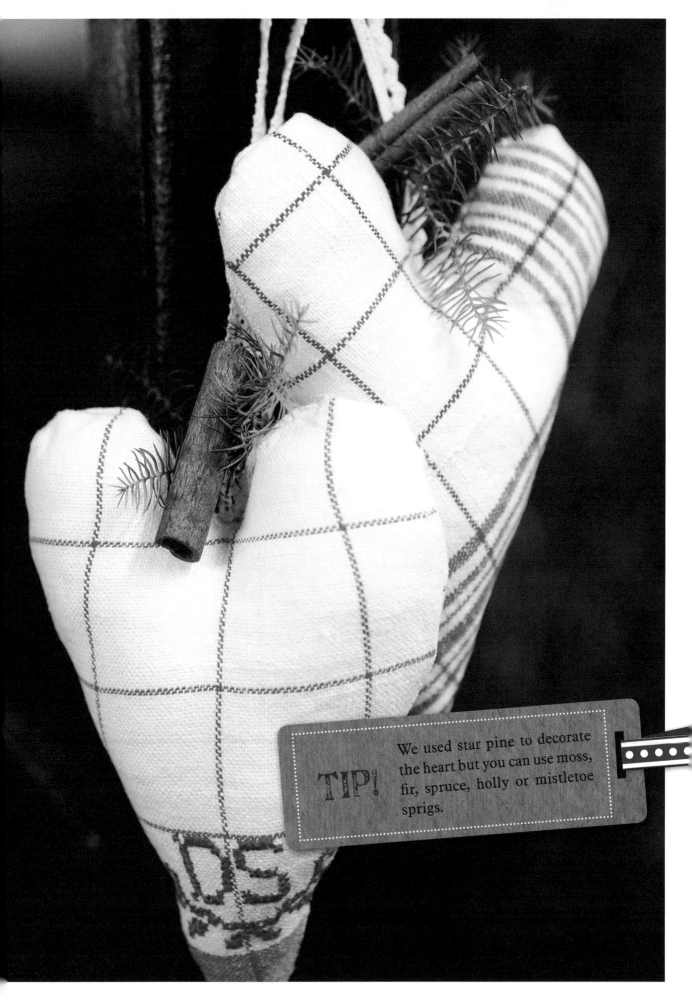

TIP! We used star pine to decorate the heart but you can use moss, fir, spruce, holly or mistletoe sprigs.

December in Bloom

There are wonderful December flowers and greenery available at the florist's. Amaryllis, hyacinth, poinsettia, cushion moss, spruce twigs and holly are just a few of the treasures waiting for you. Here are some ideas for enjoying flowers, greenery and decorative fruit throughout the festive season...

In Sweden, hyacinths are the fragrance of Christmas. Everything the flower needs is in the bulb, so don't worry too much about watering or feeding.

Hyacinth parcel

Materials: moss, hyacinths, an attractive dish, pine cones and rowan berries, thick string

Instructions
1. Wrap the moss around the hyacinth bulb and wind round the string.
2. Put this in the dish. Decorate with more moss, pine cones and other attractive items.

Cloves in oranges is the classic version. Try limes instead!

Lime pomander

Materials: citrus zester or sharp knife, metal skewer or small knife, limes, cloves

Instructions

1. Carve out decorative rows in the limes with the citrus zester or sharp knife. Or you can skip this step if you prefer (see photographs).
2. Make holes in the peel for each clove using a metal skewer, a small knife or similar.
3. Push in the cloves.

TIP! Tie a pretty ribbon around the limes to hang them up instead of putting them in a bowl. Tie the limes like a parcel – once around the middle and once from top to bottom – with a loop at the top for hanging up.

Vintage scalloped cake moulds are very pretty. I was really pleased to find a stack of them at the flea market. They make excellent flowerpots and look lovely with candles and simple decorations.

Green Christmas candles

Materials: scalloped cake mould or other pretty container, oasis block, 4 candleholder bases, 4 candles, moss, lime, spruce twigs, small pine or larch cones, steel wire

Instructions
1. Cut a lime into thin slices and put them on a baking tray. Dry in a convection oven at 50°C (120°F) for 2 hours. Leave in the oven as they cool down for a few hours or overnight.
2. Cut a piece of oasis block to fit the cake mould.
3. Place four candleholder bases in the oasis block. Add the candles.
4. Cover the oasis block with moss.
5. Position small spruce twigs around the inside edge of the mould. Secure two slices of dried lime to the small cones using a piece of steel wire.

Sugared fruit is a true classic. We make this every year using fruit we have at home. The photograph shows apples, pears, tamarillos, pomegranates and figs – but plums, grapes and lychees are also tasty.

Jack Frost fruit

Materials: egg white, fruit, castor sugar

Instructions
1. Lightly whisk the egg white.
2. Brush a thin layer of egg white over the fruit. (If the layer is too thick, it gets lumpy and the sugar won't stick.)
3. Sprinkle over plenty of sugar and let the fruit dry overnight on a wire baking rack.

Moss has to be the best plant for Christmas, and is extremely popular in Sweden. It's easy to look after and has many uses. As well as these trees, you can make balls of moss to hang at the front door.

Moss tree

Materials: 4–5 thin straight sticks, string, large Styrofoam or polystyrene ball, moss, gold wire, gingerbread hearts with a hole, oasis block, flowerpots, white stones

Instructions
1. Cut a piece of the oasis block to fit inside the flowerpot. Tie the sticks together with string and push them into the oasis block.
2. Cover the Styrofoam ball with moss, and secure it by winding gold wire around the ball several times. Use a piece of the wire to attach the gingerbread biscuit.
3. Press the ball of moss onto the sticks. Cover the oasis block with white pebbles.

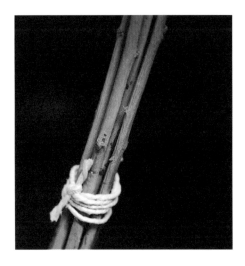

Around the Christmas Tree

Wool is a fantastic material for making Christmas-tree decorations as it's more flexible than cotton yarn. Combine slightly coarse wool with glass beads, or why not add a snout and two ears to make a cute pig?

Knitted Christmas-tree baubles

Materials: 100% wool yarn in 4 ply (US: sport weight) in your choice of colours; 75 mm (3 in) diameter Styrofoam or polystyrene balls; buttons and glass beads; cotton wool
Needles: 3 mm (UK: 11, US: 2–3); crochet hook 3 mm (UK: 10, US: C–2–D–3)
Stitch pattern: the ball is worked in stocking stitch. Increase by making 1 stitch between 2 knit stitches.
Cast on and purl 1 row in selected colour. Then work as follows:
White-red-grey-striped ball: 4 rows red, 2 white, 2 grey, 2 white, 2 grey, 2 white, 2 red, 2 grey, 2 white, 2 grey, 2 white, 2 grey, 2 red, 2 white, 2 grey, 2 white, 2 grey, 2 white, 4 red
Red-green ball (see page 84): 4 white; 2 red, 2 green (8 times); 2 red; 4 white
The pig and the grey ball: are knitted in one colour

Knitting instructions

Cast on 8 stitches, purl 1 row.
Rows 1–2: increase in the next row (knit 1, knit 2 in next stitch) 4 times = 12 stitches. Purl 1 row.
R 3–4: (knit 2, increase 1, knit 1) 4 times = 16 stitches. Purl 1 row.
R 5–6: (knit 1, increase 1, knit 2, increase 1, knit 1) 4 times = 24 stitches. Purl 1 row.
R 7–8: (knit 1, increase 1, knit 4, increase 1, knit 1) 4 times = 32 stitches. Purl 1 row.
R 9–10: (knit 1, increase 1, knit 6, increase 1, knit 1) 4 times = 40 stitches. Purl 1 row.
R 11–12: (knit 1, increase 1, knit 8, increase 1, knit 1) 4 times = 48 stitches. Purl 1 row.
R 13–14: (knit 1, increase 1, knit 10, increase 1, knit 1) 4 times = 56 stitches. Purl 1 row.
R 15–26: (knit 1, increase 1, knit 12, increase 1, knit 1) 4 times = 64 stitches.

Knit 11 rows in stocking stitch on these 64 stitches.
R 27–28: (knit 1, knit 2 together, knit 10, knit 2 together, knit 1) 4 times = 56 stitches. Purl 1 row.
R 29–30: (knit 1, knit 2 together, knit 8, knit 2 together, knit 1) 4 times = 48 stitches. Purl 1 row.
R 31–32: (knit 1, knit 2 together, knit 6, knit 2 together, knit 1) 4 times = 40 stitches. Purl 1 row.
R 33–34: (knit 1, knit 2 together, knit 4, knit 2 together, knit 1) 4 times = 32 stitches. Purl 1 row.
R 35–36: (knit 1, knit 2 together, knit 2, knit 2 together, knit 1) 4 times = 24 stitches. Purl 1 row.
R 37–38: (knit 1, knit 2 together twice, knit 1) 4 times = 16 stitches. Purl 1 row.
R 39–40: (knit 1, knit 2 together, knit 1) 4 times = 12 stitches. Purl 1 row.

Continues on next page ⋯⋰

TIP!
Knit the balls on four double-pointed needles or circular needles to avoid sewing up the back of the ball. Work all rounds in knit.

R 41–42: (knit 1, knit 2 together) 4 times = 8 stitches. Purl 1 row.
Cast off. Cut yarn leaving a long tail and pull this through the last stitch. Crochet chain stitch with this tail until it is long enough to make a loop. Fasten off and weave in this and all other ends except the one for sewing the ball together.

If you are making a pig, make the snout and the ears now. If not, put the Styrofoam ball into the knitted cover and sew the sides together with invisible stitches. Add a glass bead.

Christmas piggy bauble

Crocheted snout

Chain 3 stitches. Join with 1 slip stitch (ss) to make a ring.
Row 1: work 6 double (US: single) crochet (dc) around the ring. Begin this and every other row with 1 chain stitch (ch) and finish with 1 ss in the first stitch.
R 2: (1 dc, work 2 dc in next stitch) 3 times = 9 stitches.
R 3: (2 dc, 2 dc in next stitch) 3 times = 12 stitches.
R 4: now work all stitches through the back loop of stitch. Work 12 dc.
R 5–6: work 12 dc. Cut yarn tail and pull through the last stitch.

Crocheted ears

Chain 5 stitches
Row 1: turn and work 4 dc, beginning with the second ch from the crochet hook.
Begin this row (and every other row that does not begin with 1 ss) with 1 ch.
R 2: work 2 dc in the first crochet, 2 dc, 2 dc in the last dc = 6 dc.
R 3: work 6 dc.
R 4: work 2 dc in the first crochet, 4 dc, 2 dc in the last dc = 8 dc.
R 5: work 8 dc.
R 6: make 1 ss in the first dc, work 6 dc, skip last dc = 6 dc.
R 7: work 6 dc.
R 8: make 1 ss in the first dc, work 4 dc, skip last dc = 4 dc.
R 9: work 4 dc.
R 10: make 1 ss in the first crochet, work 2 dc, skip last dc = 2 dc. Fasten off.
Work 9–10 dc on each side of the ear. Make 2 ears.
Attach the ears and 2 buttons for eyes to the knitted Christmas-tree ball. Fill the snout with some cotton wool and sew onto the pig. Then put in the Styrofoam ball and sew up.

It's a special delight when children find sweets on the Christmas tree. Choose whichever candy your children like best.

Goody bags

Materials: cellophane bags or cellophane, invisible sticky tape, decorative ribbon, sweets or candy

Instructions
1. Use ready-made bags or cut the cellophane into pieces and make your own bags. Put the sweets in the bags.
2. Tie together with a decorative ribbon.

Crystal beads are an affordable luxury to brighten up the dark winter nights. I love them and hang several on my Christmas tree.

Crystal baubles

Materials: steel wire, large crystal bead, small white and transparent beads, decorative ribbon

Instructions
1. Cut 2 x 20 cm (8 in) lengths of steel wire.
2. Thread the large crystal bead onto one piece of wire. Twist the wire together just above the crystal bead.
3. Thread the small beads onto the second piece of wire. Join to make a ring.
4. Attach the large crystal bead to the middle of the ring of beads, making sure the large bead is close to the ring with no wire showing.
5. Make a loop with the ends of the wire from the large crystal bead to hang up the ornament.
6. Cut off of any extra pieces of wire.
7. Tie the ribbon into a bow and attach to the loop.

These need some practice to perfect, but are beautiful. This recipe makes ten decorations.

Icing ornaments

Materials: egg white, a few drops of vinegar, 250–300 g (9–10½ oz) icing sugar, castor sugar, ribbon, greaseproof paper or a piping bag

Instructions
1. Mix the egg white, vinegar and icing sugar together with a spoon. The icing should not be too runny or too thick.
2. Make a cornet out of greaseproof paper and secure with a pin so that it doesn't unravel (or use a piping bag). Fill the cornet with icing and cut off the tip.
3. Sprinkle an even layer of castor sugar onto a baking tray. Pipe the icing in the shape of a star onto the castor sugar. Leave to dry for a day.
4. The ornaments are very fragile so be careful when attaching the ribbon and hanging them up.

If you don't have a Christmas tree, why not decorate a plant pot instead, adding coloured Christmas-tree baubles?

Christmas 'tree' in a pot

Materials: oasis block, flowerpot, pine-tree branches, Christmas-tree baubles, steel wire

Instructions
1. Attach pieces of steel wire to the baubles. Cut large sections of pine-tree branches.
2. Cut a piece of oasis block to fit inside the pot.
3. Arrange the pine-tree branches and baubles in the oasis block, covering it completely.

These personalised parcels are good work for nimble fingers. Use vintage crochet or lace, or get out your crochet hook and design your own.

It takes no time at all to crochet pretty flowers and rosettes for your Christmas presents. Wrap presents in plain brown paper and personalise them. We used red and gold yarn for one flower. What colours do you like?

Gift rosettes

Materials: small amounts of woollen or acrylic yarn, glitter yarn, crochet hook suitable for use with chosen yarn

Small flower

1. Chain 3 stitches. Join with 1 slip stitch (ss) in the first stitch to make a ring.
2. Work 6 double (US: single) crochet (dc) around the ring. Start row with 1 chain stitch (ch) and finish with 1 ss in the first dc.
3. 1 ss, 2 treble (US: double) crochet, 1 ss in every dc. Finish with 1 ss in the first stitch in the row. Cut yarn and weave in loose ends.

Double flower

Use wool yarn and glitter yarn and a thick crochet hook. Follow instructions 1–3 for the small flower.

4. Turn work. Make 1 ss in the first dc in the first row *Chain 3 stitches, make 1 dc in next dc from first row*. Repeat * to * 6 times = 6 ch loops at the back.
5. Turn work again and work 1 ss, 2 treble (US: double) crochet, 1 ss in every ch loop. Finish with 1 ss in the first stitch in the row. Fasten off and weave in all loose ends.

Snowflake

1. Chain 3 stitches. Join with 1 ss in the first stitch to make a ring.
2. Chain 4 stitches. Then (1 treble [US: double] crochet, 2 ch) 5 times around the ring. The last ch loop is joined with 1 ss in the second ch at the beginning of the work.
3. Work 1 dc, 1 treble (US: double) crochet, 1 dc in every ch loop. End with 1 ss in the first dc. Fasten off and weave in all loose ends.

Double flower

Snowflake

Small flower

The linen cupboard is the perfect place to find wrapping for presents. Circular crochet covers and lace doilies are great for making little bags (see photographs pages 92–3).

Luxury Christmas bag

Materials: coloured fabric, lace or crocheted doily, decorative string or ribbon

Instructions
1. Cut out a large circle of the coloured fabric.
2. Place the circle on top of the lace. Put the present in the middle of the fabric. Fold up the edges and pull tight.
3. Wind round a piece of string or ribbon, making sure the lace is also held in place. If the lace is too small to be held in place by the string, you can attach it to the fabric with fabric glue or a few small stitches.
4. Make a pretty bow with the ribbon.

These really are pretty presents – at least on the outside. Try your local flea market for vintage lace and crocheted pieces.

Lacy parcels

Materials: wrapping paper, crocheted or lace fabric or doilies, string or ribbon, craft glue

Instructions
1. Wrap up your present in the wrapping paper.
2. Glue the lace onto the parcel.
3. Wrap the string around the parcel and tie a bow.

An advent calendar with a gift for each morning in December is very exciting for children. When my children were small I made an advent calendar to get them out of bed even when it was pitch black outside.

Advent calendar board

Materials: Christmassy patterned fabric, thick Styrofoam board (70 mm, 2 ½ in) or a cork pin board, drawing pins for the back, pins for the parcels, 24 small gifts, wrapping paper, pen, string

Instructions
1. If you're using a Styrofoam board, position the fabric on it, folding the corners over the back. Pull the fabric tight and attach at the back with drawing pins. If you're using a pin board, attach the fabric within the frame with pins or drawing pins.
2. Wrap up 24 Christmas gifts with paper and string. Write the numbers 1–24 on them.
3. Attach the parcels with the pins.

So simple – and so effective. All you need is some decorative paper and the numbers 1 to 24, for an Advent calendar made of parcels.

Advent calendar cornets

Materials: 24 small Christmas presents, tissue paper, pieces of decorative paper (e.g. sheet music, wrapping paper or comics), red paper, craft glue or sticky tape, a decorative bowl

Instructions
1. Cut up pieces of the sheet music or other paper, and tape or glue together to make cornets.
2. Wrap the small presents in tissue paper.
3. Put the parcels in the cornets.
4. Print out the numbers 1–24 on red paper, using a bold font. (If you don't have a printer you can write the numbers by hand.) Cut out circles around the numbers and glue them to the cornets.
5. Put the cornets in an attractive bowl.

Making this advent calendar is worth the effort, as you can use it year after year.

Advent calendar boxes

Materials: 24 empty matchboxes in different sizes, 24 small Christmas presents, coloured paper, glue, angel or other festive stickers, gold stars, marker pen

Instructions
1. Using the matchbox as a template, cut out a piece of paper to cover it. Fold the paper around the matchbox and glue it underneath.
2. Glue the paper to the matchbox. Leave the short ends of the box uncovered, so they can be opened.
3. Decorate the matchboxes with stars and angel stickers.
4. Number the matchboxes 1–24 and put small presents in them.

Present ideas

* Pieces of Lego
* Raisins or wrapped sweets
* Beads or pretty stones to make a necklace
* Homemade 'gift voucher' for a fun activity to do together, such as 'baking day' or 'buying the Christmas tree'
* Small wooden animals, coloured marbles, bouncy balls, etc.
* A Christmas craft project
* Trading cards

The Great Outdoors!

Choose a tree in your garden and hang up these beautiful beaded decorations. Just one little ray of sunshine makes them sparkle wonderfully.

Angels made from beads are a lovely addition to your Christmas tree or can be hung in the garden. The angel lights up when the sun shines – no electricity required.

Beaded angel

Materials: 3 pieces of 35 cm (14 in) steel wire; 2 large, transparent glass beads with a large hole in the middle; white, transparent and green beads; wire cutters and flat-nosed pliers

Instructions

1. Thread the 3 pieces of wire through one of the large glass beads. The threads should extend out further at the bottom of the bead than at the top.
2. Thread the transparent and white beads onto 2 of the wires above the large glass bead. Thread the beads 10 cm (4 in) along each wire. Shape into wings and insert the wire into the large glass bead. Use the pliers to wrap the wire underneath the pendant to keep the wings stable.
3. Thread one more large glass bead onto the wire between the wings. Twist the wire to keep the angel's head in place, then make a loop for hanging up the angel.
4. Thread the green beads (or other beads of your choice) onto 2 of the wires underneath the large glass bead, threading smaller beads onto 1 of the wires.
5. Shape the inner wire with the smaller beads into an oval and wind the wire underneath the lower large glass bead to secure. Do the same with the outer wire, this time making the oval larger.
6. Finish by twisting the remaining wire round a few times underneath the lower large glass bead. Cut off all the ends with wire cutters.

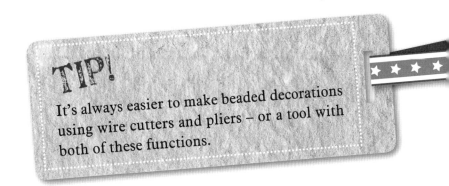

TIP!

It's always easier to make beaded decorations using wire cutters and pliers – or a tool with both of these functions.

Hearts are a Christmas classic and a shape that's easy to make. Try different styles of heart and add a crystal bead.

Sparkling heart

Materials: 35 cm (14 in) length of steel wire, 10–15 cm (4–6 in) length of steel wire, 30–40 glass or crystal beads in different sizes, 1 large crystal bead or pendant, wire cutters and pliers

Instructions

1. Bend the steel wire in the middle to make a V shape. This V is for the top, middle section of the heart.
2. Thread on the beads, 15–20 on each side. Bend into a heart shape.
3. Pull the two ends of the wire down to form the bottom tip of the heart. Wind these around several times. Thread a crystal or glass bead onto both wires.
4. Bend up and twist the ends of the wire around and secure with the pliers.
5. Thread the shorter piece of wire around the top of the heart to make a hook or a loop.

Threading beads in a row – simple and beautiful!

Glittering pendant

Materials: large, transparent glass beads; coloured glass beads; 20 cm (8 in) length of steel wire; pliers

Instructions

1. Thread 2 beads, 1 small and 1 large, onto a piece of steel wire. Twist the end of the wire up into the second bead to stop the beads falling off. If the wire is too thick, bend the wire up and twist above the first small bead (see photograph).
2. Thread the beads on in the desired order.
3. Finish by bending the wire into a hook or loop at the top.

Make a pretty, sparkling angel from beads and steel wire.

Glistening guardian angel

Materials: steel wire, glass beads – large and small, 1 crystal pendant, wire cutters and pliers

Instructions
1. Cut 40 cm (16 in) of steel wire and thread on the small beads.
2. Shape the steel wire using the template on page 127. First bend in the middle of the wire to make the head and then shape the rest of the angel. Thread on the beads in the right order before you bend the wire.
3. Twist both ends of the wire together at the bottom of the angel. Add a large bead here.
4. Thread the large crystal pendant onto both wires. Bend the wire up and wrap it round securely.
5. Finish by bending a new piece of wire into a hook or loop and attach to the top of the angel.

Pretty pictures deserve to be seen, especially frozen in ice.

Hanging ice decorations

Materials: flat baking tray, water, gingerbread or biscuit cutters, cut-out pictures, ribbon or string

Instructions
1. Boil the water and leave to cool; this will make the block of ice clearer.
2. Pour the cooled water into the tray should be 1 cm (½ in) deep. Place the biscuit cutters in the tray.
3. Put a picture into each biscuit cutter. Cut the ribbon or string into 15 cm (6 in) lengths and make loops. Place the ends of the loops into each cutter.
4. Put the tray in the freezer or outside if it's below zero (Celsius) until the water turns to ice.
5. Carefully lift the block of ice and remove the ice from around the biscuit cutters. Lift the cutters, using a little lukewarm water if they are difficult to shift.
6. Hang up in a tree outside.

We used plastic Champagne glasses from last summer to make Santa decorations.

Santa ice decoration

Materials: plastic glasses, water, glitter, Santa (or other) bookmark, ribbon or string

Instructions
1. Boil the water and leave to cool; this will make the block of ice clearer.
2. Pour water into the glass.
3. Position the bookmark on the inside of the glass. Add the glitter.
4. Make a loop with the ribbon or string and put the ends into the glass.
5. Put in the freezer or leave outside until the water has turned to ice. Take Santa out of the glass and hang him up.

Snow has fallen and the ground is covered in a thick white blanket. The trees are coated in powdered snow. Winter is at its most beautiful – and most difficult for birds. Help our feathered friends by hanging up snacks.

Gifts for the birds

Materials: small cake tins, birdseed mixture, coconut oil, ribbon or string

Instructions

1. Cut the ribbon into 20 cm (8 in) lengths. Make the ribbons into loops and place in the cake tins.
2. Melt the coconut oil in a pan. Put in enough birdseed to make a thick but manageable mixture.
3. Put this into the cake tins. Make sure the ribbon ends are inside the mixture and the loop is outside. Take out the birdseed cakes when they have hardened.

TIP! Coconut oil can be messy so put a piece of newspaper underneath the cake tins when you fill them with the birdseed mixture.

The loveliest bird feeder in town – a wooden board, with a heart of apples.

Apple bird treat

Materials: wooden board, 30 x 40 cm (12 x 16 in) or required size, black outdoor paint, heart-shaped paper template, 4–5 cm (1½–2 in) long nails, 3 kg (6½ lb) apples

Instructions
1. Paint the wooden board.
2. Tape the paper heart to the back of the board. Hammer in the nails from the back to the front in rows, with 4 cm (1½ in) spacing between them. Make sure the nails are not too close together.
3. Push the apples onto the nails on the front of the board. The apples don't need to be right in the middle of the nail but they do need to be secure.
4. Hang up the bird feeder in your garden.

Ice lanterns are incredibly beautiful and very easy to make. I used cottonseed meal, mistletoe and holly here, but feel free to decorate your lantern in other ways. Boil the water before you use it, to make the ice clearer.

Glowing ice lantern

Materials: plastic jar with lid, glass candleholder, leaves and berries, water

Instructions
1. Boil the water and leave to cool.
2. Add the first layer of water to the jar. Add leaves or other small items. Leave enough space to fit a glass candleholder on top of this layer.
3. Put the jar in the freezer or leave outside until the water is frozen.
4. Add more boiled, cooled water, more berries and plants. Put the candleholder into the middle and hold in place with the lid. Water expands when it freezes so leave a bit of space at the top of the jar.
5. Freeze again.
6. Pour water into the jar to loosen the ice block.

If you don't want to freeze the lantern in two stages, make a lantern with a hole in the middle: a cake ring mould is the perfect template.

Ringed ice lantern

Materials: cake ring mould, water, decorations such as nuts, Christmas tree baubles, berries and leaves

Instructions
1. Boil the water and leave to cool.
2. Put the decorations into the cake ring mould. Add water. Leave 1 cm (½ in) of space at the top.
3. Leave in the freezer or outside until it has turned to ice.
4. Pour water into the mould to loosen the ice block.

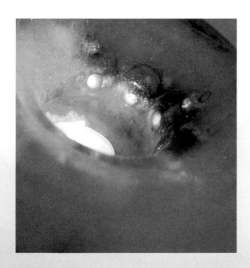
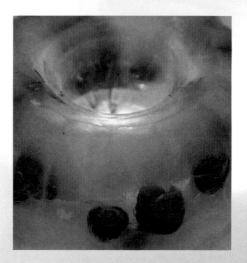

All good things come in threes, so why not hang three hearts on your door? Box(wood) is evergreen – the perfect winter decoration. Holly is also lovely and traditional in the run-up to Christmas.

Hanging hearts

Materials: 3 pieces of steel wire: 80, 60 and 40 cm (31, 23, 15½ in) long; thread, box(wood) or holly branches, velvet ribbon, thick string

Instructions

1. Shape the steel wire into hearts. Begin by making a small loop. Twist the wire below the loop to secure it. This loop is for the top of the heart (see photo). Make a V-shape with the ends of the wire. Then shape the rest of the heart. Join the wire ends at the bottom to make the tip. Make two more hearts in the same way in different sizes.
2. Cover the wire with small branches of box(wood) or holly. Begin at the top, adding small bundles of leaves to the heart. Tie the branches on with thread, leaving the thread on the bobbin. Add branches one section at a time, each time attaching them securely. Continue to the tip of the heart then cut and tie the thread.
3. Do the same on the other side. Decorate the other hearts in the same way.
4. Tie a bow with the velvet ribbon at the top of each heart.
5. Tie the hearts together with string, and use string to hang the hearts on a door or wall.
6. Tidy the leaves and bows with scissors.

Don't throw away old metal tins – use them to make lovely lanterns. These simple lanterns brighten up the dark winter nights beautifully.

Tin-can lanterns

Materials: tin cans, pen, spray paint, methylated spirits, a small metal drill or hammer and nails, steel wire, glass beads

Instructions
1. Clean the cans thoroughly with methylated spirits.
2. Draw a heart or your chosen pattern on the can.
3. Carefully make holes in the can following the pattern. Use a hammer and nails if you do not have a metal drill. Place a piece of wood inside the can to prevent it being bent out of shape. Make three holes at the top of the can for hanging up.
4. Spray the can with paint. You might need a few coats to cover it.
5. Thread pieces of steel wire through the three holes and secure them to the can. Thread on the beads.
6. Twist the tops of the wires together and thread on a larger bead. Make a loop for hanging up the can and twist the ends of the wire together to secure.

A stool made of moss is a festive decoration for your garden. Moss keeps for a long time and you can update the stool regularly using different objects. A lantern, apples or a Christmas rose all look great.

Moss stool

Materials: small stool, moss, thin metal wire

Instructions

1. Divide the moss up into fairly large pieces. Begin by covering the legs of the stool with moss and secure it by winding round the metal wire.
2. Cover the seat with one large piece of moss. Wind round the wire several times so that the moss is secure.

We've used moss again for the base of this garland; it's easy to work with and keeps for a long time. Add new leaves when the moss garland needs freshening up.

Christmas wreath

Materials: straw ring or other wreath base, moss, metal wire, ivy or holly (or other leaves and berries), thick string

Instructions
1. Cover the wreath base with moss and secure it with the metal wire.
2. Tuck in the leaves and berries underneath the metal wire.
3. Wrap thick string around the top of the wreath several times. Tie it tightly, making a loop for hanging up the wreath.

Patterns

Candy-striped glasses case

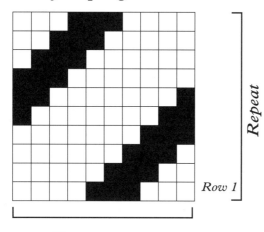

Repeat

Row 1

Repeat pattern

Scandinavian star cover

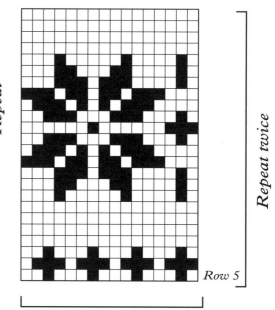

Repeat twice

Row 5

Repeat pattern

Snowflake cushion

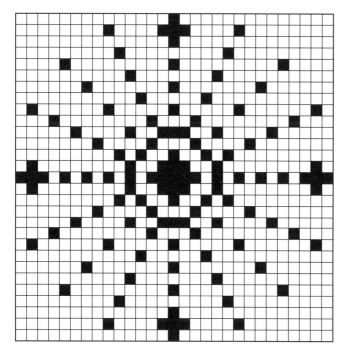

Row 17

About the authors

Freelance photographer Pernilla Wästberg and freelance journalist Caroline Wendt work mostly on articles about gardening, food and interior design. They had been working together for a while when they discovered their common interest in crafts – this book is the result. Pernilla is especially fond of gingerbread, hyacinths and moss. Caroline likes to use yarn, sparkling beads and flea-market finds.